I0712053

WORLD'S WAR

CLAUDIUS MOLLOKWU

authorHOUSE®

AuthorHouse™ UK
1663 Liberty Drive
Bloomington, IN 47403 USA
www.authorhouse.co.uk
Phone: UK TFN: 0800 0148641 (Toll Free inside the UK)
       UK Local: (02) 0369 56322 (+44 20 3695 6322 from outside the UK)

Published by AuthorHouse 06/12/2024

ISBN: 979-8-8230-8660-8 (sc)
ISBN: 979-8-8230-8659-2 (e)

Print information available on the last page.

CONTENTS

Preface vii

Historiography xi

Prelude... xiii

Chapter 1   Origins...1

Chapter 2   Early beginnings 9

Chapter 3   Adolf's Formation 15

Chapter 4   Later Formation 19

Chapter 5   War one years and early politics 34

Chapter 6   German domestics 44

Chapter 7   World War 2 55

Concluding thoughts....................................65

Postscript 67

Bibliography..73

PREFACE

I WAS INTRODUCED TO HITLER'S LEADERSHIP AND GERMAN history at my primary school where I learnt about the second world war in which she was active in. At secondary school in my final two years, I was to meet Germany's story of warfare once more.

This monograph offers me a substantive chance to revisit themes once known long ago as well as new evidence which has arisen in the past few years if not unknown.

There are many historical workers detailing the history of Hitler and Germany., most likely as an abiding reminder that 'never again' should such a war ever happen again for Europe and the rest of the world.

There are a few points I wish to make before continuing with my exposition. In short, there are discoveries I've made through my own research. These points are fairly novel and are fairly hidden in modern academia- it is this monograph's attempt to point out and discuss the new data in what I hope will contribute to further studies concerning not only world war 1 but also the aftermath of world war 1.

First, the war was about family ties- relationships became mixed up and strained between Hitler of Germany, Stalin of Russia, Chamberlain of Britain and Pope Pius xii, Bishop of Rome who all descended from the Romanov dynasty and given that they were cousins, leaders such as Stalin, Chamberlain and the Pope had mixed feelings about Hitler's plans given that they were family and did not want to kill him off.

Second, Hitler proved a capable and efficient leader of Germany. He had lots of ideas and lots of plans for how he wanted Germany to turn out following his reforms. There was no need for a war- he was just being greedy- there was plenty to do in Germany, following the sufferings she had endured from the Versailles Treaty which had imposed the reparations and had saddled Germany with enormous debt.

Third, according to some sources Hitler's intentions to Europe were firmly amicable. He did not want revenge as such for the reparations that Europe had imposed on Germany following the first world war- instead he wanted to help Europe and improve her. Hitler wanted Germany to conquer, annexe and improve norther Europe whilst Stalin and Mussolini of Russia and Italy respectively would conquer, annexe and improve southern Europe.

Fourth, Hitler began life as a bohemian. He had no political ambitions early on- he wanted to be an artist- painter and architect. He enrolled in schools and saloons at Munich and Vienna. Though initially places for Hitler to engage in artistic activities, he soon fell into a men's society and political saloon where they all debated about how to improve Germany. Hitler had found his cause and vocation- he was an enthusiastic speaker at these events and he soon decided that he would embark on a career in politics.

Finally, the war that followed after Hitler's actions would prove to be the final major war in Europe- Europe as a result fulfilled its role as a Catholic Christian supra-organisation.

I have thoroughly enjoyed writing this book. In a sense it is a collective effort. My thanks go to my primary and secondary school teachers who taught me about Hitler and Nazi Germany. My thanks also go to my editors who sharpened up the prose. Without their assistance this book may not have emerged- or at least not in the form in which it has been written. All errors, if any, remain mine. I hope you enjoy it.

HISTORIOGRAPHY

THERE ARE SEVERAL STUDIES ON HITLER AND HIS government. Christian Goeschel has traced the exclusion of his 'fascist alliance' with Mussolini. Kurt Bauer showed that he was centrally involved in the failed Austrian coup of 1934. Andrew Kramer's study of the May crisis of 1938 and its consequences showed that the 'conceptual pluralism' in Nazi foreign policy only existed at the level below the doctor himself. Rolf-Dieter Miller has persuasively argued that Hitler's plan in 1938-9 was to attack the Soviet Union, and that he was only deflected by the Polish refusal to cooperate. Ian Kershaw has emphasised the role that America played. Edward Westermann and Carroll Khol compared Hitler's war in Russia with the American West. The volumes of Das Deutsche Reich, in effect the official German history of the war, have shown Hitler's centrality to the course of the conflict. Finally Hitler's central role in the killing of 6 million Jews has been proven beyond all doubt by Richard Evans, Peter Longerich and others involved in the rebuttal of David Irving's claims to the contrary.

PRELUDE

According to the historian Norman Stone, 'the Europe of 1914 was one that was very much well and healthy. There was the Mall in London, the imperial centre of a quarter of the world's land surface; the new Hofburg in Vienna [...] the Millennium monument in Budapest; celebrating the 1000th anniversary of the Hungarians' arrival in Central Europe; the enormous Victor Emmanuel wedding cake in Rome. Paris had had the Napoleonic treatment somewhat before, and the triumphalism of the period is shown mainly in the Pont Alexandre III. If you were European or American, you were supposed to be a master of the universe, and even the lesser capitals, such as Brussels (reigning over the Congo), had their pompous display'.

Everything was going fine. Few writers were pessimistic- most believed in European progress. Authors such as HG Wells were its leaders- science would save mankind. By 1945, at the end of the second war, 'Mind at the End of its Tether,' Wells turned pessimistic. But he was wrong again- Europe as a result of the Marshall Plan fund launched in 1947 by America was spent on western Europe enabling her to emerge from the destruction that the war had caused.

Europe as a result began to flourish. Horses and carts became motorcars; hospitals became places for recovery, not death through infection or pain; film, aircraft, psychoanalysis, skyscrapers, telephones- all products of that generation. Life expectation [increased] whilst populations doubled.

Let me take a step back. Europe despite her early success fell back into war during 1915. As a result of Austria's leader, Archduke Ferdinand being shot by a Serbian terrorist, Germany in alliance with Austria was drawn into a war with the rest of western Europe. They lost and most of the blame was placed Germany. The League of Nations which was a supra-organisation of European countries that was set up after the first war that was designed to end all conflict in Europe decided to charge Germany a large set of monetary reparations though the 'Treaty of Versailles'. France in particular was at the forefront of making Germany pay. She had suffered two invasions from Germany in the last sixty years, hence she sought overwhelming revenge which was to charge Germany with large monetary reparations at Versailles. The two countries could not make up, even after the first war ended- for example, France kept a military base still in tact for fear that she might be attacked again. The responsibility to pay reparations. was an act that greatly angered Germany and the German population especially since her economy was greatly harmed.

Hitler, Germany's new idea post the Weimar Republic government which had been set up by the Republic and proved not to be so successful was to bring about recovery in Germany by enabling her to have an empire In the Est just like the American and British ones. He believed that if he threatened to invade, then the west would enable him to have his own way and even encourage him in his endeavours to attain the east.

Hence there was a second world war, after the western countries rejected Hitler's plans. Hitler proved popular amongst the German people- he had revived the German economy; the German's found him to be a powerful orator and enjoyed listening to his speeches, and no longer was Germany humiliated and impoverished by her erstwhile enemy France.

CHAPTER 1

ORIGINS

Just before the second world war there was a first world war, just as devastating and just as damaging as the first. Before going on to detail the narrative of the second war, I will first of detail the occurrences of the first war since it is directly linked to the second war. The historian Professor Margaret Macmillan has noted recently that the League of Nations policy of imposing sanctions on Germany did not cause the second war as such and did not anger the German elites causing them to launch an attack on Europe. The conventional historical view is that the imposition of sanctions upon Germany deeply angered Hitler and the Germans causing them to launch a retaliatory attack upon the rest of Europe. However there are other views- according to some other sources. For example there is the view that Hitler in alliance with his fellow fascists Joseph Stalin of Russia and

Bernito Mussolini of Italy wanted to save Europe from causing damage to itself and was keen to embark on creating policies that would do much to enhance her social and economic welfare. For example, I would note that Hitler's wish to improve Europe after the first world war- his intentions were thoroughly amiable. He sought to annexe northern Europe to the care of Germany whilst Southern Germany would be cordoned off to Stalin and Mussolini, Russia and Italy.

Of course, even before the modern 20st century there have been wars that have occurred around the world such as the one hundred years war, the thirty years war, and the wars of religion. All these have occurred in the preceding centuries though the difference between these wars and the 20th century wars is that the latter was more modern in the sense that the military and arms used were more technologically advanced posing more of a threat to the lives of the general populace in countries where the wars were going on.

Back to the first war. The Archduke Franz Ferdinand of Austria, heir presumptive to Emperor Franz Joseph 1 of Austria visited Sarajevo, capital of the recently annexed Bosnia and Herzgoviana from the movement known as Yong Bosnia, which aligned up positions along the route of the Archbishop's motorcade, with the intention of assassinating him. They believed his death would free up the annexed areas and recover once again recover their freedom and liberty. An agent and terrorist Gavrilo Princip threw a grenade at the Archduke's car and injured two of his aides who were taken to the hospital. The attack was to launch the offensive and war effort that would last from 1914 to 1918. The war has been titled as the 'Great War' and the war to end and conclude all wars but that is not strictly true- there was another war which was also to include Germany and the allies- probably just as damaging and ruinous as the first war. It has been termed 'world war 1'. There have also been other wars to rival the tragedy but none have been as serious, grievous and long lasting as the two world wars. Europe and the globe are relatively divided but for the most for the part have now accepted that we need a form of political and liberal democracy where people vote for their preferred and favourite political party which they wish to govern their country. Most countries now have liberal democracies in place and it would seem that the political academic Francis Fukuyama's 'End of History' essay has come true where he notes that after the collapse of the Berlin Wall which officially ended the cold war, political and economical liberal democracy would now once be in the ascendancy and would remain there for the remaining future. Such an article when first published caused upheaval, but it is beginning to be accepted that with a upheavals here and there for example, with the likes of the Russian-Ukraine and Israelian-Palestinian relations thgs are relatively settled with the UN dealing effectively with such wars.

Germany stepped in and as allies of Austria sought to go on the offensive in defence of the aforementioned country and province. Countries known as the Central Power, or Allies as it were, included Bulgaria and the Ottoman Empire supported Austria-Hungary and Germany fought against the Allies who were Russia, France, Belgium and Great Britain, the latter who were joined by Japan, Romania, China and the United States. The Allies won and beat the German and Austrian effort. It has yet to be known as to why despite

Germany defending Austria, Germany bore the brunt of the blame and the resulting trouble in terms of being charged with paying the reparations charged by the League. Germany was only defending Austria and was not seeking to cause any military offence to other countries hence I see no reason why it should be blamed for the mishaps that occurred in the war.

In early 1917, the United States entered the war on the side of the Allies, and in the same year, the Bolsheviks seized power in the Russian October Revolution, they made peace in the Central Powers in early 1918. Germany launched an offensive in the west in March 1918, and despite initial success, it left the German Army exhausted and demoralised. A successful Allied counter-offensive later that year caused a collapse of the German frontline. By the end of 1918, Bulgaria, the Ottoman Empire and Austria Hungary agreed to armistices with the Allies, leaving Germany isolated. Faced with revolution at home and with his army on the verge of mutiny, Kaiser Wilhelm II abdicated on 9 November.

In terms of the war, 9 million soldiers died, 23 million wounded, plus another 5 million civilian deaths from various causes. Several millions more died as a result of genocide and the war was a major factor in the 1918 Spanish flu pandemic.

The war ended with the Armistice of 11 November 1918, whilst the subsequent Paris Peace Conference imposed various settlements on the defeated powers, notably the Treaty of Versailles. The dissolution of the Russian, German, Austro-Hungarian, and Ottoman Empires resulted in the creation of new independent states, including Poland, Finland, Czechoslovakia and Yugoslavia. Despite the aforementioned powers losing their territories they would soon recover their powers and clean up the environment economically and socially.

After the war, a collaborative effort titled the League of Nations was convened after the Paris Peace Conference ended the war. The league was a supra-organisation that contained a worldwide collective country of nations. As well as charging Germany a large sum of money as recompense for the war- that is to say reparations- the League installed a new governing system within Government known as the Weimer Republic. However under the system the Republic underwent several problems. For example, the country suffered hyperinflation with the occurrence of the Great Depression in 1929 as well as political traumas with the end of Chancellor Mueller's grand coalition and the beginning of the presidential cabinets. From March 1930, President Paul Von Hinderburg appointed Hitler as Chancellor in coalition and led with the Nazi party to head a coalition government.

The League and the resulting Weiburg Republic as government in Germany that resulted from it was a complete failure. Germany became economically and socially crippled- her government and governance deteriorated. Such a situation was to last until Hitler and the Nazis achieved power through authoritarian means and embarked on a legislative program that would improve Germany's economy and ultimately society. Germany under the reforms of Hitler and the Nazis recovered. Her recovery was successful- all the reforms were carried without the assistance of the other European powers who allowed Germany work out and figure out things for herself. There was an economic miracle where Germany enjoyed infrastructure and economic reforms and improvements. For example there was economic success where autobhans-long road express ways were built whilst the likes of new mini cars such as the Volkswagens were built and became part of everyday mobile life for the German people to navigate the autobhans. The vw's also were an international success- they were transported and sold to many countries. The country became well developed through a series of strict policy and developmental policies issues. Hitler ran a state socialist government- authoritarian- in short autarky- absolute power where the government had absolute and total control command and central control over the economy and the means of production, spending money on the private sector in order to stimulate private sector businesses in a bid to make the economy grow. The economy enjoyed decent growth and Hitler wanted to spread Germany's success to other European countries hence his wish to annexe other countries to his own country, Germany.

Hitler and the Nazis ascended to power using relatively conventionally democratic means and when the party began to govern they did so in a legitimate manner that was also democratic with the exception of the 'krishalnacht' otherwise known as the 'putsch' where Hitler and his henchmen of SS troops made their debut in German frontline politics by storming the political centre streets. The Putsch was a sign that Hitler and his party would destroy Germany's reputation as well as the rest of Europe by throwing Europe into war though Europe after the war including western Europe recovered with the help of Russia and America, though these two latter countries would take on the mantle of 'superpowers' who fought against one another in a 'cold war' across the global world including countries such as Cuba, Vietnam and Hiroshima. The world had not yet learnt its lesson- global countries despite being funded by Russia and America are still engaged in military warfare. It would take until 1990 when the Berlin wall collapsed as well as President Mikail Gorbachev's policy of 'Glasnost' and 'Perotroika'- 'Openness" and 'Transparency' for war to officially end. There has never been a repetition of war yet.

However that is not to say that wars around and across the world have not ended. It is just that wars have been relatively short and relatively sharp. In the 20th century there have been wars in the Middle East including the Kuwiet-Iraq war, the Afghan-America war in response to the September 2011 attacks, the Anglo-Iraq war, the Anglo-Kosovo war, the Anglo-Libyan war, the Anglo-led Iraq war and the Arab-Israeli war. At the time of writing there are two wars on two fronts- Russia has not learnt her lessons and is flexing her muscles in in her decision to invade a series of countries such as Crimea and more recently Ukraine. Meanwhile, Israel has invaded the Palestinian territory of the West Bank. There are now wars on two fronts of the world. Having said that supra-organisations such as the United Organisations are beginning to organise various countries world wide to deal with issues concerning the problems their governments and general populace are facing in terms of being militarily being targeted.

This book is a narrative of how one leader, one party and one country caused massive trouble around the would, arguably without any intention yet negligently. Such a few- history as narrative is beginning to be once again accepted especially in academic history. Whilst I accept such a view- that is not the only the view- for example, there is history as analysis which in modern times has been taught in the academy where events in the past are scrutinised and reach a conclusion based on an interpretation of evidence and the facts. History as analysis is beginning to be criticised and held up as 'faux history', however such a discipline continues to be relevant for academic history- there is space for both disciplines- narrative and analytic- I see no cause or reason for either to be rejected. Through my research and use of sources available to me at the time of writing I have come to the view that the war was caused by one of incidents, incompetence and one in which it was caused by the League of Nations establishment of the Weimar Republic which was not democratic as such but was a despotic power that governed Germany poorly. It would take until the Nazis' arrival in power before everything would be fixed economically and socially but even then they ruined it and caused trouble for themselves through invading the Czech Republic and later Poland hence causing war with Europe and the west. Europe as of yet- western and eastern has yet to recover. There are still areas- scenery and economically that have yet to recover.

CHAPTER 2

EARLY BEGINNINGS

Adolf Hitler was born an Austrian to a German family by historical accident on April 1889. His birthplace, Braunauam Inn, was part of the Duchy of Bavaria for hundreds of years before being ceded to the Habsburg monarchy at the Treaty of Teschen which concluded the War of the Bavarian Succession in 1779. In of his familial background it was progressive and fair minded- a far turn from what Hitler would descend intro. His father, Alois Hitler's, freethinking liberal thought as regards the Roman Catholic Church- he was neither disloyal to the Hapsburg, anti-Semitic, drunken or violent towards his children.

Adolf's family came from the countryside, from the Waldviertel, a district of woods and hills in Lower Austria, in between the Danube and the Bohemian frontier, where the name Hitler, possibly Czech hailed from in term's Hitler's ancestors who were peasants, but not serfs, small independent farmers or village craftsmen. There is even evidence that the Hitler family hailed were an aristocratic family whose lineage goes back centuries.

Alois proved to be an ambitious man in his family. By the time in 1855 he was eighteen, Alois had gained employment at modest means but still at a level worthy of an aristocrat at the ministry of finance. For a young man of his background and limited background, his advancement was somewhat impressive. After training, he qualified as a banker. His income was secure and he attained a social standing worthy of the rank of his job and education- when he passed away he left his family an income that would secure them. He was very much the master in the house, a quality that would influence Hitler's governance of Germany and the early years of the war effort when Germany was winning. The family life that Adolf led was far from harmonious and happy- Alois was pompous, status-proud, strict, humourless, frugal, pedentrically punctual, and devoted to duty. He was highly esteemed by the community, though internally with the family he was a dominating husband- this is not really supported by Hitler whose view in 'Mein Kampf' was one of sufferance- he was neither poor nor harshly treated.

Adolf was a younger child in a large and mixed family. By the time of Adolf's birth, Alois, his father managed to achieve promotion and a solid substantive salary. He had an older brother, Alois Jnr, and a half-sister, Angelo, from his father's first marriage to Franziska's Matzelsberger. After her death he married his cousin with whom he had a further six children, of whom only two survived, Adolf and his younger sister Paula. Two of his four siblings died before he was born and one when Hitler was nearing ten's year old. Klara's sister Johanna, nicknamed 'Hinitante', was a major figure in their lives. Alois worked several miles away from home- - after retiring to Leonding he collapsed and died over a morning intake of wine in a local hostelry on 3 January 1903.

The widowed Klara moved the family first to Linz and then to Urfahr on the other side of the Danube.

Whatever harshness they received from their family, this was more than made up for with the affection shown from their mother Klara. It was not as such a happy home at the Hitlers. Hitler's younger sister Paula notes that 'it was especially my brother Adolf who challenged my father to extreme harshness and who got his sound his thrashing every day...How often on the other hand did my caress him and try to obtain with her kindness what the father could not succeed [in obtaining] with harshness. For his father and him there would be between the two outbursts of temper'. Meanwhile, she notes that for his mother, she was deeply concerned about the beatings that Adolf was receiving from his father, sometimes waiting outside the household door as he was thrashed. Another issue is that there was violence between husband and wife in what was a rancorous home.

According to her Jewish doctor, Dr Bloch, after his own forced emigration from Nazi Germany, Klara Hitler was a 'simple, modest, kind women. She was tall, hall, brownish hair which she kept neatly plaited, and a long, oval face with beautifully expressive grey-blue eyes'. In character, she was submissive, retiring, quiet, a pious church taken up in the running of the household, and above all absorbed in the care of her children and stepchildren. Adolf was close to his mother- Dr Bloch, his mother's doctor notes, 'Outwardly, his love for his mother was his most striking feature'. He later wrote, 'While he was not a 'mother's boy' in the usual sense', he added, 'I have never witnessed a closer attachment'. I one statement of affection for his mother, he notes in 'Mein Kampf', 'I had honoured my father, but loved my mother'.

Misfortune after misfortune befell the family- Adolf's father collapsed on 3 January 1903 after his usual glass of wine, in the Castlaus Wiesinger, the conflict of will over Adolf's future was over. There was no a struggle between Adolf and his mother over Adolf's planned intended vocation no that his father no longer proved an obstacle to his intended vocation. His last two years of schooling proved mediocre and he often feigned illness to his mum in what was a careless disregard for his education.

Just up to going to higher education, Adolf led a life that was comfortable and cocooned, surrounded and comforted by many female members of his family including his mother, his aunt Johanna, and his little sister Paula who were all there to look after him. The historian, Ian Kershaw notes that his family were there to wash, clean, and cook for him during a period of idleness in his own room in the impressive family flat in the 'Humboldtstrale' but my sources note that they were only there to cook as well as providing conversation as is when naturally flows. In support of her son's ambitions, Klara bought her son a grand piano where he had lessons for four months between October 1906 and January 1907. These days for Adolf were one of comfort and ones in which he sought to immerse himself in culture- he spent his days drawing, painting, reading, or writing 'poetry'- the evenings were for attending the theatre or opera plus he spent all of his spare time dreaming about his upcoming life as an artist. He stayed up later into the night and slept long the morning. This period of laxity was called by Hitler, 'the happiest days which seemed to me almost like a beautiful dream'.

In early 1907, Hitler's mother after a short illness in which she was diagnosed with cancer passed away. She was looked after by her surgeon Dr Eduard Bloch, a Jew. Hitler treated him with kindness and never forgot the fact that he had looked after his mother. He did not blame Dr Bloch nor became an anti-semite and he even gave him a hand painted card wishing him a happy new year. Later on Hitler allowed Bloch to flee Austria, whilst keeping the main Jews stuck on mainland Germany where they were subjected to massive ill treatment the cause of which had never yet been seen or has not been seen again.

In 1913 Hitler left Vienna for Munich in a bid to avoid military service in the Habsburg army. A year later, he was caught up with by the authorities where had to undergo a magistrate's hearing, although military service proved academic since he was discharged as he was regarded as being physically unfit. He then returned to warfare- he volunteered for the Bavarian Army, serving with some distinction at the Bavarian Army.

Hitler as well as Bloch had friendly relations with two other Jews where in Vienna he canvassed his paintings: the Moravian Jew Siegfried Loffner, who ws a suspect and questioned by the police in the alleged Hanisch fraud, and the Hungarian Jew Samuel Morgenstern, who kept a careful record of these purchases. From what the sources tell us his time in Vienna was spent in busy activity where his interests were architecture, town planning and music, especially the connection between such interests and subjects. Hitler regarded himself as an 'artist' in the Stumpergasse in mid February 1908, as a 'student' in the Felberstrasse in mid November 1908, as a 'writer' in the Sechshauserstrasse in late August 1909, and as a 'painter' at the Meldemannstrasse in early February 1910 and again in late June 1910.

'Mein Kampf' work remains Hitler's sole autobiography and testament of his life as well as a testament of his political and social views. It dealt with foreign affairs, Esperanto, pets and public speaking. His earlier antipathy toward Britain relaxed and he believed their empire should remain whilst Germany should expand their territory at the expense of Russia. Hitler departed from the russophlie empire, which had kept the Bolshevick Revolution, but retained a maintained an animosity against France – though being Prussian, he did not utter much or anything about the country, though such a country would chaos and echoes of warfare once it marked the beginning of the world.

'Mein' deals with the 'Hottentots and 'Zulu Kaffirs' as close to social treason. Basically it was Social Darwinianism fused with -pseudo-Nietzschean. It was here that he was to formulate his programme of eugenics with regards to unwarranted violence and abuse on Europe and the Jewish people of which 6 million passed away. He even went as far as to note that his theory of eugenics with regards to war could be a good force for regeneration and reboot with the general populace- the war which Hitler launched was regarded as 'the bloodiest civil war have often rise to a stealthy and healthy people.

CHAPTER 3

ADOLF'S FORMATION

Alois Hitler made a final move of home to a village on the outskirts of Linz where he bought a house with a small plot of attached land in Leonding, a village on the outskirts of Linz. For Alois this was to be the most stable place in which he would live and in which he would work as a banker.

Adolf's life at elementary school was promising- he was bright and showed early promise.

By this time, Adolf was in his third year of elementary school. He seemed to have gained many friends and was the 'ringleader' in games of cops and robbers which the collective played in the woods and field near their homes. War games were an especial favourite and Adolf was especially enthused by the illustrated Franco-Prussian War which he came across at home. He also around this time came across the adventures of Karl May, popular tales of Wild West and Indian wars captured the young imagination of the young Adolf. Indeed one could note that these talehood films captured the imagination of Adolf and would give some notes with regards to how to later lead Germany and further on how to lead the war. For Adolf, the works of Karl May would never fade- as Chancellor he continued to read them, recommending them to his generals in a bid to cause them to raise their game. Adolf later referred to 'this happy time', when 'school work was ridiculously easy, leaving me so much free time that the sun saw of me than my room', when 'meadows and woods were then the battleground on which the ever present 'antagonisms'- the growing conflict with his father- 'came to a head'.

Far from the joyful happy days of his elementary education, Adolf's secondary years were more difficult. He failed to make out-of-school friendships due to the one hour trips to and thro from school. His classmates took little notice of him and he had no close friendships and neither did he seek any. Also the attention he had received from his primary school teachers was now received by teachers who gave him a more formal and informal less or even no pastoral form of education. His school work as compared to that of his elementary suffered and his behaviour tended to the immature rather than the diligent that had previously defined him.

After trouble with his elementary school, his mother tried to send him to a boarding school in Steyr, but such a move proved ineffective, and did little to alter his work pattern. By the time he left in autumn 1905, his school record had declined significantly recorded at poor and mediocre. Adolf notes that his adolescence was very painful which the move from elementary to secondary school had marked a 'very painful' effect. His school too had little regard for him and described him as idle, wilful and disrespectful. The happy, playful youngster of the primary school days had grown into an idle, resentful, rebellious, sullen, stubborn, and purposeless teenager.

In a letter to counsel, during Hitler's defence counsel concerning Hitler's role at the Putsch, his former class teacher, Dr Eduard Huemer, noted Hitler as a thin, pale youth commuting between Linz and Leonding, a boy not making full use of his talent, lacking in application, and unable to accommodate himself to school discipline. His teacher seems to have had a sneaky regard for his pupil- he notes that was noted as stubborn, high handed, dogmatic, and hot-tempered. With his classmates he was domineering and a leading figure in playing pranks.

Regarding Hitler's response to his teacher, he too did not hold them in high regard. He did not enjoy his school and teachers with the exception of one and left 'with an elemental hatred' towards it, and later mocked them. Dr Leopold Potsch, his history teacher was singled out for praise in 'Mein Kampf' though his exciting narratives of Germany's nationalist past and anti-Hapsburg past.

A lung infection incurred in the summer of 1905 enabled him to persuade his mother that he should give up his time at school and aim to gain a place at at the Vienna Academy of Arts. He put off taking the exam for two years, enjoying the years of self freedom and leisure time years that he gained.

Supported by his mother, without the stern rod of his father, he spent two lazy years of whiling the away preparing the time as an artist who would impress and stun the outer world.

It now came to the time when Adolf would choose what type of education he would have. He chose to pursue a course in Art which was met with significant displeasure at the hands of his father- 'Artist, no, never as I live'. Hitler chose to have an arts and humanities education at the School of Arts at Vienna from which he was barred from. After passing the first test where a third passed out of 111, Hitler too also joined them. However by this time his drawings were graded 'unsatisfactory' hence he was not amongst the twenty-eight candidates allowed to pass through. This was a blow to Hitler- he had always been confident that he would pass the exams- he notes in Mein Kampf', 'convinced that it would be child's play to pass the examination…I was so convinced that I would be successful that I when I received my rejection, it struck me as a bolt from the blue'. After attending the university to enquire why they had rejected him given that his talents lay in architecture, he left the interview 'for the first time in my young life at odds with myself'.

CHAPTER 4

LATER FORMATION

Hitler moved to Vienna in 1908 and borrowed a large sum of money from his 'Hanitante' in order to fund his living expenses whilst he also supplemented this by his orphan's pension. He applied several times but to no avail. Hitler began the low ascent upwards up and away from the lower orders when he moved to the well-suited Men's Home. He lived there for three years and the locus provided a place for him to complete his paintings and postcards, copied from prints rather than the organic open air. Contrary to what would later occur later on, he had close and friendly relations with all the Jews that he met.

Hitler met a friend Auguste Kublicke who was to remain with him as a good friend for a substantive term of Adolf's formation. They lived together and shared the same lodgings. Their first place of residence in Vienna was a room in the

Stumpergasse. Their landlady, Maria Zakreys, was Czech and by Hitler's account she spoke imperfect German. Hitler at this time were very cultural- music and architecture. In February 1908 he announced his intention to purchase a piano though this exuberance subsided when his landlady Maria rejected the piano wish and promised to purchase a viola instead, leaving Hitler crestfallen. However he got over both wishes, and began to occupy with other events informing Maria, 'I am now writing quite a lot, normally in the afternoons and evenings'.

Hitler's education at the Staats Realschule Linz continued. The school was known for its German nationalism and anti-Hapsburg views- to views that would vehemently and violently influence Hitler in his years as leader and chancellor of Germany. After doing well in his early years at the school, he began to care less ardently about his education securing high marks only in drawing and sports. There was no sign at this point that he was interested in politics- he joined various organisations- cultural, namely- the Linzer Musealverein, the Oberosterreichischer Musikalverein and the Oberosterrechischer Volksbildungsvrerein- but apart from that there is no sign at that age of political engagement. There is also no sign that he met his fellow student Ludwig Wiggenstein who was to become an acclaimed philosopher. Either way Hitler is. Regarded as a low quality student, forced to repeat a year before leaving school at 15.

He gained help from several people and patrons who sought to fund his education.

It was also at this time that Hitler was beginning to be intellectually and politically agile. He attended different events that were occurring in the German, European and global affairs. One view discerned was that ethnic Germans were being swamped by the Slavic majority of the multi-national Austro-Hungarian empire; another was that assimilated Jews were too conspicuously predominant, while unassimilated eastern Jews, fleeing successive pogroms in the Tsarist empire, were part of the Slavic inundation. A sense of German beleaurgment was exploited by Pau-German nationalist politicians, who wanted the ethnic German Austrians to out of what they regarded as the multinational 'zoo' of the Habsburg empire, to join up with their mighty Teutonic southern neighbour, leaving the South Slavs in the Balkans to kill each other. Very few Germans shared this first enthusiasm, not least because it would mean that German shared this first enthusiasm, not least because it would mean that German Protestants would be outnumbered by Roman Catholics'.

A writing saloon in the Men's Home provided reading materials and a seminar for the many in-house autodictats. At night Hitler in his cubicle, rather than mixing with soldiers, working men and Czech serving girls in Vienna chose to focus on reading materials by himself. He was well behaved and chose not to drink or smoke and did not dance. Though he claimed to be a construction worker, Burleigh notes that such a view is very much unlikely since his lack of physicality makes such a view not so. His reading is difficult to ascertain. Since newspapers and pamphlets published noted the 'representative' thoughts of any number of writers and thinkers, it was easy to give the impression of wide erudition and of high scholarliness. He was especially sympathetic with authors, like him of Vienna's academic and intellectual community who were self-conscious outsiders. He held those whom he read in high regard. There were several rings of authors on the looser ends of decency such as Aryans or scientific doctrines such as 'world ice teaching'.

A key figure in Hitler's early formation years was August Kubizek

It was around this carefree time in Hitler's lifetime in Linz between 1905 and 1907 that August Kubizek was with Hitler during said time. Kubizek was a close friend and diarist of Hitler and whilst much of it need to be treated with care especially when balanced for accurateness when it comes to putting it up against 'Mein Kampf' it is still relatively source worthy. August Kubizek- 'Gustl'- was some nine months older than Adolf. They met by chance in autumn 1905 at the opera in Linz, especially the works of the 'master of Bayreuth', was shared Kubizek. Both- August and Adolf had balanced and opposite characters and attitudes. August was highly impressionable, Adolf out for someone to impress. August was compliant, weak-willed, subordinate; Adolf was superior, determining, dominant. August felt strongly about little or nothing; Adolf had strong feelings about everything. 'He had to speak', recalled Kubizek, 'and needed somebody to listen to him'. For August, having attended a lower order school and believing himself to be socially and educationally inferior yet despite being from just as privileged background as Hitler placed himself second to Hitler- Hitler would often harangue him- blasting off issues and opinions of the day. It was a partnership that worked perfectly well and both became the best of friends with August providing moral succour to an at times wayward Adolf- the loss of such a friend as times moved on deeply wounded Adolf and caused pain to Germany, her leader and then the global world in terms of the damage that the war caused to worldwide countries.

As well as sharing a love of music a theme that motivated both Adolf and Gustl were together, was great art and architecture. August was the more working class of the two- he worked in his father's workshop. Adolf spent his leisure time in drawing pieces and works of artist. George Buth spent there night at the theatre and opera. Hitler was especially well turned out. Both were highly caught up in the music especially to those of Wagner. Hitler highly desired that August join him in living at lodges despite August's parents refusal. One postcard reads- 'Dear friend ', 'am anxiously expecting news of your arrival. Write soon so that I can prepare everything for your festive welcome. The whole of Vienna is awaiting you'. A postscript again: 'Beg you again, come soon'. Four days August's his parents bade him a tearful goodbye where he left his parents to join Adolf in Vienna where he would support his friend in his all his endeavours.

Hitler sought to apply to the arts academy, the Vienna Conservatoire but was rejected first time round. His friend however, August got through- relations between the two would never be the same again.

For the second time Hitler applied to the academy but preparations were just as bad as the first one- once again his study partner was Kubilev and whilst Kubilef gave him the necessary attention- ideas that erupted and often dissipated once thrown up into the year., it was not enough concerning

Hitler's career. He failed once again to gain entrance into the Conservatoire.

There now appeared to be a change in relations between August and Adolf with the prior overtaking in intellectual and practical dominance over the latter- things became frosty. Between the two. August's wholistic and stead educational background readily free of mishaps and comfortable middle class lifestyle overtook Hitler's more difficult background no matter how precocious Hitler was in his youth. For August it was a slow ascension- he had bided his time, letting Hitler get it all out of his system- overexerting himself before declaring his own intentions. Kubizek within the next few days learnt that he had been accepted at the Vienna Conservatoire. He rented a grand piano which occupied much of the double room just allowing Hitler to do his stomping- a sign that August was finished with such act- it would no longer be tolerated. August was making his presence felt- he fitted in two beds, a commode, a wardrobe, a washstand, a table, and two chairs.

August set into a regular music study pattern which was not supported by Adolf. August was flourishing whilst Adolf was floundering. Hitler during this time was aimless- he was often in bed or missing during August's return from the Conservatoire. He was probably and most likely sulking over his friend's activities in the academy- whilst he was stuck with nothing to do- it would have hurt even more given that the Conservatoire was Hitler's discovery and his idea- all stolen by August- something which they had a row over. He spent free times at salons, drawing painting, reading, drawing. When a row erupted between the two friends 'What now, what now?...Are you starting too: what now?'.

'Hitler had a dangerous education'- one that would reverberate not only in Germany but around the world. Though not antisemitic during and shortly his birth, he became an antisemite within two years of arriving in Vienna. He spent three years at the Men's Home which he spent in and one in which he undertook his education filled with activity reading antisemitic newspapers, pamphlets, and cheap literature. According to Karl Hanisch, Hitler had no views or accounts of Jews though he did have views on the 'Jesuits' and the 'Reds', though makes no comment on any hatred of Jews, though he certainly joined in talk about the Jews in Men's Home. Hanisch notes that Hitler had always admired the Jews for their resistance to persecution, praising Heine's poetry and the music of Mendelsson and Offenbach, which expressed the view that the Jews were the first civilised nation in that they had abandoned polytheism for belief in one God, blaming Christians more than Jews for usury, and dismissing the stock-in-trade of Jewish ritual murder as nonsense.

Basically for the most part, Hitler was self-educated. However his failure to achieve a formal higher studies did not as much have a significant effect on him. His self-directed studies would prove suitable for preparing him for his leadership of his adopted country, Germany where he combined his consultation of cabinet which echoed his early friendship with August with his ability to take decisions on his own independently of cabinet which echoed his own free time away from August as well as his free and leisure time spent at the Men's Room, reading materials that most likely provided him with policy ideas that would help him govern Germany.

Hitler during this time was aimless- he was often in bed or missing during August's return from the Conservatoire. He spent free times at salons, drawing painting, reading, drawing. When a row erupted between the two friends 'What now, what now?...Are you starting too: what now?'. The sole truth was Hitler had no idea where he was going or what he would do. He was drifting aimlessly. Apart from architecture, Hitler's main passion was music the likes of Beethoven, Bruckner, Liszt, and Brahms. He greatly enjoyed as well the operratas Johann Straus and Franz Lehar. Together he and August saw operas by Mozart, Beethoven, and the Italian masters Donizetti, Rossini, and Bellini as well as the main works of Verdi and Puccini.

In terms of the Men's Room's, it provided a period a space for quiet study and work feeding Hitler's mind with ideas that would soon find fruition in his governance of Germany and in the war. Whilst August was gone in the morning, he stayed in bed, hung around the grounds of Schoborn Palace on fine afternoons, pored over books, fantasized over grandiose architectural and writing plans, and spent a good deal of time until later into the night. Hitler was also active with activities unbeknowest to his friend during the night. It was also around this time that he read books, pamphets and articles by philosophers such as Houston Stewart Chamberlain, Charles Darwin, Friedrich Nietzsche, Gustave Le Bon and Arthur Schopenhauer.

For the most part, Hitler fell on hard times. With his savings depleted he was forced to move to shabbier accommodation nearby Sechhauserstra for less than a month. He stayed for said month before departing on 16 September, leaving the area without filling in the required police registration form, without a forwarding address, and probably without paying his rent. During these times, Hitler being far away from home and family, learnt the bitter lessons of living in poverty. He noted that autumn 1909 was 'an endlessly bitter time' was not an exaggeration. His finances and savings were depleted and were no more. Hitler had reached rock-bottom. In the weeks before Christmas 1909, he arrived, poor and destitute at a place for homeless people. The once chance student was now with people who had little chance of professionally or socially succeeding. He couldn't even enjoy the simple tidings of Christmas.

However all was not lost. It was at this time that he met Reinhold Hanisch, who was to become a close friend of his and with whom he would forge a professional and friendly partnership. After August, Hitler was in good and well company with Hanish. They met in a hostel offering night sheltering. A bath, shower, disinfection of clothes, the two new aquaintances shared soup and bread. Hanish offered a job to the down and out Hitler to help him earn some money for living expenses- first to shovel and eliminate the snow that had fallen that Christmas, but Hitler did not have suitably warm clothes to cope with the cold. Next up, Hitler offered to carry bags for passengers at the Westbahnhof but his appearance probably meant he received few customers. Hanish began to be upset with Hitler for his relaxed attitude to getting a job. When Hitler told Hanish of his time as an art student at the Academy in Vienna, Hanish came up with the idea of Hitler selling paintings of Vienna. His Aunt Johanna gave him 50 Kronen which he used to purchase himself a decent warm coat. Hitler now looked neater than before- a long coat, a greasy trilby,, shoes that imitated those of a sojourner, hair over his collar, and dark fuzz over his skin. The two- Hitler and Hanish were set to go with their new venture- they never looked back.

With finances now in place, Hitler moved to the Men's Home which was a significant improvement from the Meidling hostel. The 500 or so residents were not down and out vagrants- they were for the most part mixed individuals- clerks, even some former academics, some just passing though tough times, others just passing, others looking for work or temporary employment, all without a family home. Residents had their own private cubicles which they could stay in at night but vacated during the day. The Home was hospitable and was well provided for- there were meals and alcohol-free drinks provided in canteens. There was a kitchen where people could cook their own meals, a series of washrooms and lockers for private belongings, the bathrooms had baths along with a cobbler's, a tailor's and a hairdresser's, a laundry, and cleaning facilities, as well as a small library on the ground floor as well as the first floor lounges and a reading room which contained the daily newspapers. Most of the men were out during this time, but around fifteen to twenty men stayed behind to use the aforementioned literary services for their own intellectual pursuits. They used smaller work rooms known as a 'working room' and a 'writing room' where they gathered and undertook piece meal work such as painting advertisements, writing out addresses as well as other things.

Hanisch and Hitler set up localities where they would plan their ventures.

Hanish's job was to promote Hitler's mainly postcard paintings in the local pubs, selling them to all those interested. He also found interest from frame-makers and upholdersters who requested cheap illustrations. Most of the deals where Hitler attracted interest from Jewish businesses- a section in society who Hitler would later treat in society with devastating cruelty once he became Germany's leader. According to Hanisch Hitler believed that his Jewish customers were more reliable than his Christian ones. He also had a Jewish business partner, Josef Neumann, also a Jew involved in his art production businesses and the second closest partner after Hanisch.

With such an educated group, matters turned to politics which was often discussed in the reading-room of the Men's Home amongst intense debates being the orders of the day. Hitler himself took full part. His attacks on the Social Democrats caused trouble with some of the inmates. He was known for his admiration for Schonerer and Karl Hermann Wolf (founder and leader of the German Radical Party, with its main base in the Sudetenland). He also praised the likes of Karl Lueger, the social reformist, but antisemitic mayor of Vienna.

When not discussing politics, Hitler would engage his fellow colleagues on his love for and the wonders for Wagner's music and the impressiveness of Gottfried Semper's designs of Vienna's monumental buildings.

These events began to distract Hitler from his main task of painting and selling through Hanisch. The latter became frustrated at the former's lack of productivity. Previously they were selling one piece of artwork a day at a competitive rate- now the work had a dried up.

Following a windfall payment from one piece, Hitler left the home for a few days with another acquaintance, Neumann spent their time sight seeing in Vienna and looking around museums. They returned a few days later both to the Men's Room and to Hitler's business partner Hanisch. Trouble would soon come the two's way in terms of a breakdown in their relationship. Through a Jewish intermediary and another associative in the Men's Home Siegfried Loffner, Hitler accused Hanisch of withholding 50 Kronen of payment for a work that Hitler completed as 9 Kronen for a watercolour. Matters were brought to the police and Hanisch was sent to jail for a few days where he used the false name of Fritz Walter. Hitler would never again set eyes on his friend again.

Two years slipped by without any record of Hitler's whereabouts, yet when we see capture him again, he is still at the Men's Home, now a established member of the community- he found a set of friends of whom he was the central figure- the 'intelligentsia' who occupied the writing-room.

Hitler, prior to past experiences led a fairly solitary life. He led a frugal life, he spent fairly little in the Men's Home, he ate cheaply, did not drink, smoked a cigarette only rarely and a rare luxury gift purchased a standing-place at the theatre or opera. There are contradictory opinions about his appearance at this time from his fellow residents at the Home. One in 1912 notes that he was shabbily dressed and unkempt, wearing a long greyish coat, worn at the sleeves, and battered old hat, trousers full of holes, and shoes stuffed with paper. He still had shoulder length hair. On the alternative, according to the Jacob Alternberg, one of his Jewish art dealers, Hitler took care to keep his hair cut, and wore clothes which, though old and worn, were kept neat.

Hitler came into a windfall from the life savings of his Aunt Johann in the province of 3,800 Kronen yet this did not make him that happy. The gloom was enhanced when his half-sister, Angela, still looking after his sister Paula, soon in 1911, staked a claim on the whole of their Aunt's finances still divided at that time between the two. Adolf who 'on account of his training as an artist had received substantial sums from his aunt, Johanna Polzl', noted that he was in a position to finance himself and hence was forced to give up 25 Kronen a month which he had up to then received from his guardian. Despite smaller gifts from his Aunt, there is no evidence that he received further finances despite one major one of 924 Kronen which was more likely a gift than a loan.

According to Karl Honisch, Hitler led a fairly unsettled life at the Home following the loss of Hanisch. Honisch describes him as slight in build, poorly nourished, with hollow cheeks, dark hair flopping in his face and wearing shabby clothes. However that does not seem to be true- Hitler led a settled life- even a joyful one at the Home. He was rarely away from the home- he could be found pretty much every day in the reading cubicles reading, drawing and painting. Everyday he would be in the same space, working away zealously and others would tell potential occupants who wanted his space that 'this place is taken'. Hitler was seen as an unusual artist and he noted that 'I believe that those who knew me in those days took me for an eccentric'. He could be withdrawn, steeped in his work or reading a book- he kept a distance and as Hornisch noted, though well regarded, he had a way, noted Honisch, of keeping his distance from the others and 'and not letting anyone come too close'.

Politics was a frequent talking point at the Home. Hitler had strong political views known to all- he would often at the beginning of a discussion, sit quietly, whilst putting in a word or two, but otherwise continuing with his painting or drawing. If a point came up that piqued his interest he would jump up, toss aside his brush or pencil on the table, he would forcibly make his point, break off mid-flow, and at the incomprehension of his comrades, take up his drawing. Two subjects were of interest to him at this time- the Jesuits and the 'Reds'- no mention was made against the Jews. Hitler's criticism of the Jesuits suggests that his enthusiasm for Schonerer's vehement anti-Catholicism was still fervent. His antipathy towards the Social Democrats was also well established. In 'Mein Kampf', he notes of difficult relations that he experienced when he refused to join them including physical and emotional abuse which he received when he refused to join a trade union when he employed at a building site handled by the Social Democrats.

The years that Hitler spent in the Men's Home gave him every opportunity to look over antisemitic newspapers, pamphlets, and cheap literature. According to Honisch, Hitler at this point in time had strong views on 'Jesuits' and the 'Reds' but his views on antisemitism are not yet known. Hitler certainly joined in discussions concerning antisemitism at the Home, but his standpoint according to Hanisch was not negative. For Hansich, Hitler admired the Jews for the resistance to persecution, praising Heine's poetry and the music of Mendelssohn and Offenbach, expressing the view that the Jews were the first civilised nation for abandoning polytheism for belief in one God, blaming Christians for usury more than the Jews. Only Josef Greiner, of those who claimed to have witnessed Hitler at first hand in the Men's Home, speaks of him as a fanatical Jew-hater in that period. For Kershaw though, Greiner's testimony is 'worthless'.

Hence there is no evidence that during this period Hitler was antisemitic. If Hanisch is to be taken seriously, Hitler was not at all antisemitic during his time at the Home- when with his comrades during the First World War, he voiced no antisemitic comments. This does not tie in with Hitler's own autobiography, 'Mein Kampf' where in 'Mein' he notes that he became antisemitic in Vienna.

His 'Mein Kampf' autobiography notes his transition from an artist to a political afficianado. Through his bitter experiences from his time at the locums for homeless people where he was poorly dressed and poorly looked after to his ascension to a more amenable environment stocked with reading materials and where he made he many friends, Hitler became a person suitably prepared to be leader of Germany. His leadership would prove to be tragic- not only for Germany, but for the world as through one man's governance, she would experience a tragic loss of citizens.

On 24 May 1913, Hitler, carrying a light, black suitcase containing all his materials left the Room and headed to leave Vienna and headed for Munich. The Vienna years were now over.

CHAPTER 5

WAR ONE YEARS AND EARLY POLITICS

As part of World War I, Hitler was decorated during his service in the Germany Army. In 1919, he joined the German Worker's Party, the anticipator of the Nazi party, and in 1921, was appointed leader of the Natzi Party. In 1923, he sought to seek electoral power by a failed coup in Munich and was sentenced to five years in prison, just serving of his prison sentence. Whilst there he dictated the first of his biography's, 'Mein Kamgf'. After releasing it, he then attacked the Treaty of Versailles and promoted, pan-Germanism, anti-Semitism, and communism as part of Jewish conspiracy.

Hitler enthusiastically involved himself in the first world war. According to a 1925 Bavarian report, Hitler's involvement in the war was most likely an error. This error was fatal- Hitler's experience gave knowledge to him about military tactics and how to organise and engineer a war which resulted in his causation of the Second World War which he nearly won especially as the historian, Max Hastings notes, a one week period in which Germany was exceptionally successfully and looked likely to win the war outright.

During his service he engaged himself In some artwork, drawing cartoons and instructions for the local army newspaper. He did not escape physical harm- he was injured in the left thigh at the Battle of the Somme. Hitler thoroughly enjoyed his time in the war effort and called it the 'greatest of all experiences' and was praised for war efforts by his commanding officers. Germany lost the war. Germany was dealt with a heavy hand by the allies for its part in the war. One point that has yet to be resolved is why Germany were so heavily dealt with in the sense that it was Austria that was first attacked- what could Germany do but defend her cousin country. However one could note that Germany became too worryingly ambitious in terms of the landed territory that she sought to gain- she used the attack on Austria as an excuse to further her territorial gains. The Treaty of Versailles was imposed on Germany- it imposed monetary reparations on the country and the Germans especially opposed Article 231, which they interpreted as holding Germany responsible for the war.

After the war, Hitler returned to Munich- he had no formal education and no formal qualifications and no carcer prospects hence he remained in the army for the time being. Hitler was assigned to an army post in the 'Reichswehr' (reconaissance unit) where he was instructed to influence the army officers there and to inlfiltrate the Germans Worker' Party. At one meeting, the Party Chairman, Anton Drexler was impressed by Hitler's oratorical skills and gave him a copy of his pamphlet 'My Political Awakening' which contained anti-semitic, nationalist, anti-capitalist, and anti-marxist ideas. Seeing the potential of Hitler for a career in politics, on the orders of his army superiors, Hitler joined the party.

Dropping his earlier sentiments, Hitler became worryingly anti-semitic. His very first essay on the Jewish issue displayed his distance and even rejection of the Zionist cause- in a letter to Adolf Gemlich, now known as the Gemlich letter, he argues that the aim of the government 'must unshakably by the removal of the Jews altogether'.

At a meeting of the party, Hitler met Dietrich Eckart one of the party's founders and a member of the Thule Society. He became Hitler's mentor exchanging ideas with his protégé and introduced him to a wide range of Munich society. The party changed its title to the 'National Socialist German Workers' Party', known as the 'Nazi Party'. Hitler too contributed- he designed the party's banner of a swastika in a white circle on a red background.

On the 31 March 1920, Hitler was discharged from the army was given the rest of his time to work for the party. The party's headquarters were in Munich, a city Hitler was very familiar with. The city was filled with anti-government German nationalists determined to eliminate and undermine the present government, the Weimer Republic. Hitler soon gave a reputation for being a passionate and intense orator and public speaker- - in February 1921 where there was already crowd manipulation, a technique the Nazis would continue to use for the rest of its spare time, Hitler spoke to a crowd of over 6,000 people. To publicise the meeting, two truckloads of party supporters drove around swastika flags and distributing leaflets. Hitler during those time gave passionate polemical speeches against the Treaty of Versailles, rival politicians, and especially against Marxists and Jews. It was a space that no one filled at the moment in time in terms of public speaking- it was only Hitler who had the courage to put himself forward and engage in public speaking at most rallies organised by the Nazi party organisers.

Early followers of Hitler who saw his potential to be a competent leader of Germany included Rudolf Hess, former air force Hermann Goring and army captain Ernst Rohm. Rohm became in charge of ensuring political meetings of the Nazis ran efficiently where meetings ran without trouble and where political opponents were dispatched of.

The Nazis with the inclusion of Hitler became more professional. The party issued a 25-point programme on 24 February 1920 which was not so much a manifesto or ideology but a bulletin list of points setting out the party's views at that point in time. The programme was mainly influenced by ideas from the Pan-Germanic movement, such as ultranationalism, opposition to the Treaty of Versailles, distrust of capitalism, as well as some socialist ideas. He also saw the program as the basis for propaganda and for attracting people to the party.

Hitler sought to enlist the help of the world war 1 General Erich Ludendorff for an attempted coup on the government known as the 'Beer Hall Putsch'. The Nazis presented itself as a fascist government inspired by fascist Italy. Hitler wanted to emulate Benito Mussolini's 'March on Rome' of 1922by staging his own coup in Bavaria, to be followed by a challenge in to the government in Berlin. Hitler's sojourn was fairly lonely in the sense that he was not supported by other leading figures in the party- despite the support of Ludendorff, Gustav Ritter von Kahr refused to join in- he had his own group-Khar, along with Police Chief Hans Ritter von Schiffer and General Otto von Lossow, wanted to install a nationalist dictatorship without Hitler.

On 8th November 1923, Hitler and the SA stormed a public meeting of 3,000 people organised by Khar in the 'Burgerbraukeller', a beer hall in Munich. Interrupting a speech by Khar, Hitler in a barnstorming speech noted that a national revolution ad began and declared a new era with a new government with Ludendorff at the forefront. Khan and his fellow cohort were present at the meeting, and Hitler and Ludendorff both convinced Khan and his followers to join Hitler's new government. At that very same meeting however, Khar and his followers reneged on the deal. Neither the army nor the police support Hitler's efforts at convening a government- they wanted to set up their own dictatorship. The next day, Hitler and his followers marched from the beer hall to the Bavarian War Ministry to throw out the Bavarian government, but the police dispersed them. Sixteen Nazi members and four police officers were killed in the failed coup.

On 11 November 1923, Hitler was arrested for high treason. After a trial in a People's Court in Munich which began in February 1924, Alfred Rosenberg became temporary leader of the party. On 1 April, Hitler was sentenced to 5 years imprisonment. He was treated well- he was given a grace and favour flat. He stayed for a year and it was here that he wrote, 'Mein Kampf'- 'My Life'. After a year, Hitler was released on 20th December 1924. 'Mein Kampf' was part biography and part manifesto with the latter setting out Hitler's plans for Germany should he and the Nazis be elected to power to govern the country. 'Mein Kampf' was published in two volumes in 1925 and 1926 where it sold 228,000 copies between 1925 and 1932. One million copies were sold in 1933, Hitler's first year in office. Shortly before his parole, the German government tried to remove him from Germany and send him home back to his homeland of Austria. Austria his own homeland refused, perhaps sensing, given his anti-democratic and anti-semitic views that he would prove if allowed once again into Austria a problematic handful. They rejected him on grounds of his service for the German military in the war, rather than serving for his own homeland of Austria. In retaliation, Hitler renounced his Austrian citizenship on 7 April 1925.

Hitler's lapse into the Nazi party and the National Socialism- he got to the top by perfectly legal means and governed by despotic yet also legal means – path to power. Hitler's Putsch- on one night on 8-9 November Hitler and his coalition hoped to match into Berlin but they were prevented by troops by the police. The Munich force clashed with Nazi stormtroopers as they marched into the city centre. The police killed more than a dozen of Hitler's supporters. This event became known as the Beer Hall Putsch. Hitler started from perfectly legal means of achieving power to illegal means of governing the country illegally through his use of the SS and SA as well as Joseph Goebels and use of propaganda to control the news and media. He had aspirations as an artist supported by his friend but he was to achieve greater things in terms of his position in the country.

After a year in prison Hitler was released, Politics in Germany had become less combative in Germany and the economy had improved. Duty to the Putsch the Nazis and their affiliates in Bavaria were banned. In a meeting with the Prime Minister of Bavaria Adolf promised to respect the state's authority and henceforth to seek power only through the democratic process. The meeting enabled the ban on Hitler and the Nazis to be lifted on 16 February. Hitler had still not learnt his lesson- he gave an combative speech on 27 February and was again banned by the authorities from public speaking. The ban remained until 1927. Despite the ban, Hitler's ambitions was not settled- he appointed Gregor Strasser, Otto Strasser and Joseph Goebbels to organise and enlarge the Nazi Party's presence in northern Germany. Strasser took a more independent course, affirming the party's socialist roots. The stock market crashed in America 1929 which had a ripple effect across the world. Germany too suffered- millions became unemployed and several banks collapsed. The Nazis promoted themselves as saviours of the country and promised to rebuild the economy, repudiate the Versailles Treaty and provide jobs.

France occupied the Rhineland in Germany in retaliation for German's refusal to pay financial reparations which the allies had imposed on it after the first war. By this time, Hitler had control of an army- the SA which he agreed to place under army command in the event of a French attack. To that extent, the NSDAP, National Socialist German Workers Party was already part of the established. Hitler was the party's main public speaker and propagandist.

Hitler at this time was still an unknown quantity. He was still unknown in most of Germany- the main Berlin ignored him and his party- they didn't even report on the riotous 'Deutscher Tag' at Coburg, whose resonance was confined to south Germany. Hitler had very few funders outside of Bavaria with the exception of the baron, Fritz Thyssen who gave a significant amount of funds in 1923. Hitler was well known in the Bavarian rightwing nationalist milieu where Hitler enjoyed a leading commission. He was well known in Munich, his place before travelling to Vienna which Thomas Mann described in a 1923 letter to the American journal The Dial as the 'city of Hitler'. Hitler's practice in public specking at the Room began to come to fruition- his speeches drew large and enthusiastic crowds. Karl Alexander von Muller who heard him speak for the first time at the 'Lowenbraukeller' in late January 1923, describes the 'core of hypnotic mass excitement' created by the flags, the relentless marching music and the short warm up speeches by lesser party figures before the man himself amid a row of salutes turned up to make the main address. Hitler would then be interrupted at almost every sentence by tempestuous applause, before departing for his next engagement.

The party fronted by Hitler over the next few months became more and more popular with increased crowds who attended to supported the speeches of leading Nazi figures. In 1923 there were in excess of 20,000 NSDAP members at the start of 1923, and that figure more than doubled over the ten months to 55,000; the SA, on the paramilitary wing of the

Nazis nearly quadrupled from around 1,000 to almost 4,000 men. Hitler became and was so close to the party that in some quarters the NSDAP became known as the 'Hitler Movement', the term which was used by the Bavarian police monitoring and recorded by them. He was now a cult figure- almost messianic in his promise to Germany for strong leadership. The Volkischer Beobachter became a daily paper in February where preference was given to advertising Hitler's speeches. Two months later it began commemorating his birthday, an honour accorded no other Nazi leader. The German people he noted needed a dictator and 'are waiting today for the man who calls out to them Germany, rise up [and] march'. Hitler was soon emerging as the sole favourite leader not only of the Nazis, but also as a potential future leader of Germany. Most were realising this. The Oberfhurer of the SA, Hermann Goring, proclaimed him at his birthday rally on 20 April 1923 as the 'beloved Fuhrer of the German freedom movement '. Alfred Rosenberg described him simply as 'Germany leader [Fuhrer]'.

Hitler was surprisingly enlightened when it came to his views on the Catholic church and the need for fairness and justice in the country. 'We want', he noted 'to see a state based on true Christianity. To be a Christian does not mean a cowardly turning of the check, but to be a struggle for justice and a fighter against all forms of injustice'. The NSDAP did succeed in terms of winning over a significant faction of the peasantry whilst some catholic clerics such as Cardinal Faulhaber also supported him before moving away. Pope Pius, known as 'Hitler's Pope' was soon to be put in a difficult position- the catholic church was not in favour of Hitler's war, yet Pius was Hitler's brother- how could he support a war that put his own flesh and blood in danger and potential loss of life. Nevertheless the Pope was honourable- he put the good of Jesus roman and catholic church before personal interests. Hitler too did not find favour with the Bavarian aristocracy, which firmly remained firmly focused on the Wittelsbach dynasty, especially Crown Prince Rupprecht, a credible figure on account of his role as a commander in the war.

During this time, Hitler was developing his plans for Germany's economy. He provided a foreword or what he called a 'catechism' in Gotfried Feder's book. He wanted an 'anti-capitalist' economy that was pro-socialist where the state had control of most of Germany's assets as well as control of her manpower. The movement was monitored by the Bavaria police.

CHAPTER 6

GERMAN DOMESTICS

THE GREAT DEPRESSION PROVIDED A POLITICAL OPPORTUNITY for Hitler. Germans were fairly unhappy with the parliamentary republic they had which faced opposition and pressure from right and left-wing extremists. The Weimar republic as It became known was unable to deal with the extremists- the referendum of 1929 helped to elevate Nazi ideology. The elections of September 1930 resulted in the break up of a grand coalition and its replacement with a minority cabinet. It's Chancellor of the Centre party was Heinrich Bruning governed through emergency decrees from President Paul von Hindenburg. The Nazis rose to prominence and became the second largest party in parliament winning 18.3 percent of the vote and 107 seats in parliament.

Hitler made an appearance at the trial of two fellow members of his affiliate party- two Reichswaur officers,

Lieutenant Richard Scheringer and Hanns Ludin, in late 1930. Both were charged for being affiliated to the Nazi which at time was illegal. The prosecution argued that the Nazis were an illegal party, causing defence layer, Hans Frank to defend Hitler. On 25 September 1930, Hitler testified that his party would pursue political power mainly through democratic elections which won him many supporters in the officer corps. Bruning's economic reforms and inflation were unpopular causing Hitler to take advantage by noting that his party would help farmers, war veterans and the middle class.

Though Hitler had terminated his Austrian citizenship meaning that he was stateless. He did not acquire German statesmanship for almost seven years. This meant that he was unable to attain public office and risked deportation. The interior of Brunswick, Dietrich Klagges, who was a member of the Nazi party, appointed Hitler as administrator for the state's delegation to the Riechsrat in Berlin, making Hitler a citizen of Brunswick, and thus of Germany.

Hitler chose to model his governance of his own party and the country by the means of Italy's fascist Benito Mussolini. In latter years he would drag Mussolini into the war that was eventually going to take place.

Hitler ran against Hindenburg in the 1932 presidential elections. A speech to the Industry Club in Dusseldorf on 27 January 1932 won him support from many of Germany's most powerful industrialists. Hindenburg's support was major- various nationalists, monarchists, Catholics and republican parties and some social democrats all supported him. Hitler used the campaign slogan 'Hitler over Germany'- in what was most likely a double quiet humorous reference and allusion to his political ambitions and his campaigning by aircraft in which he was one of the first politicians using that mode and form of travel. He came second in both rounds of the election garnering a substantive 35 percent in the final rounds. Though he lost to Hindenburg Hitler had firmly established himself through the elections as a force to be reckoned with.

The absence of an effective government prompted two influential politicians, Franz von Papen and Alfred Hugenberg, along with several other industrialists and businessman, to write a letter to Hindenburg calling for Hitler to be appointed leader of Germany and head of a government 'independent from parliamentary parties' which could turn into a movement that would 'enrapture millions of people'. Clearly these two advocates believed that Hitler had the ability to govern Germany effectively and restore her back to her days of greatness.

Hindenburg agreed and after two further elections in which there was no outright winner, Hitler was appointed to lead a short-lived coalition government formed by the Nazi party which had the most seats in the Reichstag and Hugensburg's party, the German National People's Party (DNVP). On 30 January 1933, the coalition was sworn in during a brief ceremony in Hindenburg's office. The Nazis gained three posts- Hitler was named chancellor, Wilhelm Frick- Minister of the Interior, and Hermann Goring Minister of the Interior for Prussia. Hitler assumed control of appointments in order to gain control over Germany's police force in much of the country.

'At the risk of appearing to talk nonsense I tell you that the National Socialist movement will go on 1,000 years...

Don't forget how people laughed at me 15 years ago when I declared that one day I would govern Germany. They laugh now, just as foolishly, when I declare that I shall remain in power' (Adolf Hitler to a British correspondent in Berlin, June 1934).

Having achieved full control over the legislative and executive branches of government, Hitler and his allies began to show their true colours. Despite promising to reach government and government according to the democratic process, they were now exhibiting their dictatorial tendencies- they sought to eliminate all forms of opposition, purging the country of any faction and section that was anti-Hitler and anti-Nazi. The Social Democratic Party was made illegal and its assets were seized. While many trade unions were in Berlin for May Day activities, SA stormtroopers occupied union offices around the country. On 2 May 1933, all trade unions were required to dissolve and their leaders arrested in what was a series reneging on Hitler's promise to protect and enhance worker rights as a way to deal with the Depression. Some were sent to concentration camps. The German Labour Front was formed as an umbrella organisation to represent all workers, administrators, company owners, thus reflecting the concept of Nazism in the spirit of Hitler's 'people's community'.

Hitler rid his government, party and the country of all remaining political opposition. By the end of June, all of the parties had been disbanded, including in what was an ungrateful act, the Nazi's coalition partner, the DVNP. With the SA's assistance Hitler forced its leader Hugenberg, to resign on 29 June. On 14 July 1933, the Nazi party was declared the only legal political party in Germany. Not even members of his own paramilitary wing were safe- in what became known as the Night of the Long Knives, Hitler in an act of mindless violence, purged the entire leadership of the SA from 30 June to 2 July 1934. Nazi propaganda presented the killings as a preventive measure against an alleged imminent coup by the SA under Rohm- the so-called Rohm Putsch. Hitler targeted the likes of Ernst Rohm and other SA leaders who, along with a number of Hitler's political adversaries (such as George Strasser and former chancellor Kurt von Schleicher), were rounded up, arrested, and shot. While the international community and some Germans were shocked by the killings, many in Germany supported their leader and believed was faithfully restoring Germany back to full order. It is believed that some 85 people were killed but others have cited that it was 700 to 1000.

As head of state, Hitler automatically commander in chief of the army, immediately after its former leader, Hindenburg's death, Hitler assumed the role in what was a growing sign of Germany becoming a dictatorship under Hitler's sole leadership. All swore allegiance to the new commander.

Despite the despotism or even dictatorship, Hitler gained power by democratic means. He and the Nazis campaigned diligently, immersed themselves in the democratic process and passed legislation using the normal channels of the German legislature or through executive orders. He also governed according to the dictats and means of the constitution hence proving his regard for German history and German politics.

Hitler was ambitious for German society and its economy. He intended to carry out a number of reforms that would transform and modernise the economy, making the country more hospitable for the country's citizens. He had lots of ideas for improving German society and the economy. In terms of the political spectrum, Hitler was left- even centre left- a national socialist if you will, the latter which his party used to call themselves. One could even identify the government as a social democratic one. He was a sensible centraliser who believed in the power of the state and the necessity of the state to own the means of production and to use those means to produce items, goods and services that would assist German society and enable her economy to thrive and flourish. Germany once again became an economic power and enjoyed times not witnessed since the times of her leader, Otto Von Bismarck. She recovered from the losses endured during the first war as well as income received from the stoppage of the war reparations imposed on the country by the League of Nations. As well as the state he was also a believer in the power of the private sector to assist the state in areas such as manufacturing roads and cars.

As well as ruling with his party, he would often and regularly after the day had finished in his grace and favour home, stand out in the porch where he would reflect over the day's events and would reflect over his policies and plans for the country which he and his government would enact.

First up on his in-tray was making boosting the car industry by creating a 'people's car' just like America's whose staple car was the 'Ford' car. He lamented that 'whereas there were about 23 million cars in circulation in America, with another 3 to 4 million being produced every year, Weimar Germany had managed to put only about 450,000 on the roads and had produced about a tenth of that number in recent years. He called upon the German car industry to create an affordable open to everyone. One particular car that proved popular during Hitler's time was the Volkswagen- or the VW- a relatively small mini car that was easy travel in. As a result of Hitler's legacy, Germany after his years in charge in modernity became a leading car manufacturer where she produced prestigious and popular cars such as the Mercedes Benz and the BMW. All of Germany's cars manufactured at this point were of a high and good quality.

If there were to be an increase in cars, it stood as logic that there had to be more roads which could contain the extra number of cars. German manufacturer and road builders began to build what became known as 'autobhans' or what is known as expressways which were long stretches of roads connecting distant areas. These roads were a success and proved popular in terms of usage.

Next up, Hitler sought to improve the aircraft industry. The British and Americans were well ahead not only in military and naval but also in domestic aviation. Hitler agitated for the increased of air travel predicting that 'in a few years nobody would even consider undertaking travel of more than 500 kilometres in anything, other than an aeroplane'. He sought to put a large airport hub at the centre of his plans.

Another area where Hitler sought to compete with and imitate Anglo-American products is the production of wireless radio sets. In 1933, Germany only had 4.3 million sets out of a population of 66 million sets, which was a lower number than America and Britain. Goebbels, galvanised some 28 private sector companies to mass produce radio sets. The combined efforts resulted in a 'people's receiver' which was presented at the German 'Radio Fair' in Berlin in August 1933. Hitler used the radio as a way to spread his propaganda and his plans for the country noting through an associated poste that 'all Germany hears the Fuhrer'. According to the historian, Brendan Simms, that is not quite true- according to him, no more than about 25 per cent would have the radio set to do so. In a sense the whole project was enlightened- the Germans had the opportunity to listed to a wide range of channels rather than just one, enabling them to acquire the news, knowledge and occurrences of what was going on not just in Germany but also outside in the broader world.

Hitler was very much interested in improving the leisure and cultural pursuits of the German people. To this end, Hitler relied on the promotion of music to achieve this, especially his favourite composer, Richard Wagner, whose ideal of an artistic Gesamtkunstwerk- embracing the aural, the spiritual and the intellectual had particular appeal. Hitler as a guest of honour at the commemoration at the Leipzig Gewandhaus to mark the fiftieth anniversary of the composer's death. At the foundation of the Wagner monument Hitler praised the composer as a man who 'embodied the best of our people' and called for 'coming generations of our people to be drawn into the magic world of this powerful sound poet'.

According to Simms' views, Hitler's artistic tastes were conservative. Some Nazi figures such as Goebels took a liking to modernists such as Emil Nolde, Edvard Munch and Ernst Barlach, all of whom were considered part of new 'Germanic' art. Hitler however had no interest in them. He preferred Brocklin, Mackart, Feuerbach and Spitzweg, all painters still highly regarded in these present times.

Even if he was conservative, Hitler was still liberal and open minded when it came to popular culture especially by promoting cinema films and music that the German people could enjoy. He did not ban Hollywood films or foreign productions- most if not all were still available to German consumers. Even Hitler himself personally liked watching films produced Hollywood.

Hitler himself intervened in the cinematic industry- a growing sign of his intervention in the private lives of the German people. For example, he attended the International Film Congress which met in Berlin in 1935 where he sent a welcoming message and gave a private audience to the leaders of the various international delegations. He announced his hope that the 'high cultural mission of film' would help to 'deepen mutual understanding among nations'. According to Simms, he notes that this was code for in the industry to avoid films sponsored by Jews which would complicate Nazi Germany's relations with the outside world.

Another policy that Hitler set out to enact was a successful agrarian and farming industry. For Hitler, the German agricultural industry was still way behind the Anglo-American one. That Autumn of 1933, he and Herbert Backe set up the 'Imperial Nourishing Estate', whose immediate task was to set agricultural prices; hence ending the free market in this sector. He saw the new policy as building up a new generation of healthy and well nourished citizens, building up a new German elite- a 'new aristocracy from blood and soil', as Darre put it in his seminal text on the subject

In terms of the economy, Hitler appointed Hjalmar Schacht as Minister of Economics and in the following year as

Plenipotentiary for War Economy in charge of preparing the economy for the ensuing war. The number of unemployed fell from 6 million in 1932 to fewer than 1 million in 1936, Hitler oversaw the infrastructural reforms to the country including the construction of dams, autobhans, railroads, and other civil works. Wages were slightly lower in the mid to late 1930s compared with wages during the Weimar Republic, whilst the cost of living increased by 25 per cent. The average work week increased during the shift to a war economy; by 1939, the average German was working between 47 and 50 hours a week.

Germany thrived socially and economically as a result of Hitler's reforms. He was full of ideas as to how he and his government could improve Germany- he knew the plans and policies needed to rescue and heal Germany from the Weimar times. He stopped paying reparations to the allies hence immediately increasing by a massive margin Germany's financial income, now that she was no longer saddled with debt.

Now that he was in power, Hitler kept a tight grip on his power. He had a band of people who were really just glorified thugs- the SA and the SS. The SA was the first body unit guard and did most of the duties regarding a unit of its type- they were integral to the rise of Hitler and the Nazis. They violently enforced party norms and attempted to influence elections. They soon lost favour and most of their power to the SS, though it did not disband until the war ended in 1945.

There was also the SS which Hitler ordered to be created just after his release from prison in Lasenberg which was to succeed the SA and fulfil the latter's main functions. The SS began life as the elite bodyguard unit of Hitler before growing into a larger a unit that had the authority to attack others without means or regard to the rule of law.

He even tightened his grip on his own supporters. For example, he engaged in a purge of his paramilitary unit, the SA in an event in what became in what became known as the Night of the Long Knives, when the SA's then leader Ernst Rohm was arrested and executed. Nazi propaganda presented the murders as a preventive measure against an alleged imminent coup by the SA under Rohm- the so-called Rohm Putsch. It is believed that some 85 people were killed but others have cited that it was more 700 to 1000.

The SA continued to exist but was superceded by the SS. It remained in existence until the Nazis downfall in 1945 at the hands of the Allies in 1945, after which it was disbanded and outlawed by the Allied Control Council.

There was a major event concerning the Germans and the Jews. The event is known as 'Kristallnacht' (Crystal Night) which comes from the shards of broken glass that littered the streets after the windows of Jewish-owned stores, buildings, and synagogues were smashed. The foundation of the event lies in the assassination of the German diplomat Ernst von Rath by Hershel Grynspan, a Polish Jew living in Paris. The event annoyed the increasingly antisemitic German population. Using the SS and SS the Germans destroyed all items Jewish- over 7,000 Jewish businesses were damaged or destroyed, and 30,000 Jewish men were arrested and incarcerated in concentration camps. The event was to anticipate the Holocaust in the Second World War when Hitler placed people of Jewish descent into concentration camps and killed approximately 6 million of them.

CHAPTER 7

WORLD WAR 2

I N TERMS OF THE WAR THAT HITLER AND THE NAZIS CAUSED, some say the war was caused by the fact that Hitler never forgave Europe, particularly the League of Nations a supra-organisation collated of the allies post world war 1 for imposing reparations on it which proved damaging and hurtful to the economy. That is the standard view amongst most if not all historians.

Another way according to a historian is that Hitler had purely kind intentions for Europe- he wanted to make Europe great again. In this project, he enlisted his fellow cousin Joseph Stalin of Russia from the same Romanov dynasty as well as the fascist Bernito Mussolini of Italy. For Hitler, Germany would try and annexe northern Europe whilst the aforementioned leaders- Stalin and Mussolini would annexe together southern

Europe. According to Hitler all three would try to collaborate and inspire Europe to achieve her former glory.

Hitler messed up- big time. Germany was doing perfectly well on her own- socially and economically- I see no reason why he wanted to invade other European countries- he was being greedy- Europe was perfectly at peace with itself- they had even absolved Germany of its reparation obligations. His annexation was wholly illegal- he was disrespecting the sovereign nature of all of the countries that comprised Europe.

Having said that Germany despite the bright start was slowly being led into being a dictatorship- Hitler had reneged on his earlier to abandon his earlier despotic path to power and to continue with his later democratic means including his soft democratic governance. He led the German people into a dictatorship from which it would be hard to retreat from. Having said, Hitler was popular- even the Jews who would come to suffer the most in the country and the ensuing war, held Hitler in high esteem- an affection not reciprocated by Hitler who had long term issues with antisemitism and Zionism.

Europe was once again for the second time in the twentieth century on the brink of war.

Hitler made it clear that he would invade and annexe Czechoslovakia as well as his home country of Austria. All in Europe were worried- England the most. Discussions about the potential war reached England's Parliament. The British Prime Minister, Neville Chamberlain was sent with a delegation to Germany to hold talks with Hitler with his plans. The two were cousins hence negotiations were fairly smooth. Hitler agreed at the behest of his cousin that Czechoslovakia would be the first and last territories to fall under German rule. He was allowed to keep Czechoslovakia.

All in Europe and wider were pleased with the result- Chamberlain came back to England a proclaimed hero and announced that Europe and the world had 'peace in our time'. Other politicians such as Winston Churchill did not as such believe Chamberlain's negotiation victory and still feared that Hitler was not to be trusted and would not stick to the agreement.

The three- Hitler, Chamberlain and Stalin were all cousins and were all part of the Romanov dynasty- Hitler included. If that is so, that explains Chamberlain's appeasement program- he could not launch an attack against his own cousin and it took Stalin a while to change his mind and join the western allies to side against his own cousin and bring Hitler and Germany down. Having said that, one cannot understand Hitler's plans- Britain and her empire under the leadership of Chamberlain was under Romanov rule as well as Stalin's Russia- so too was Hitler, himself a Romanov had a grip and hold of Germany which he kept under Romanov rule. If that is so, a substantive amount of Europe was still under Romanov rule- even if it was in the form of a more democratic or despotic guise.

Even the Pope- Pope Pius xii of the Roman Catholic Church was related to all the aforementioned- despite the church being a church that wanted peace, was fairly in his opposition to the war, though affirmedly against the plans of his relations still sided with the allies and their quest to defeat Hitler.

Churchill proved to be correct- on the 1 September 1939, Hitler and his allies invaded Poland.

This time the western allies had enough- they attacked Germany and her allies- Italy and Russia in a bid to defend her territories. Germany for the most part was engaged in a bitter war with France. Britain helped and concentrated her efforts on rescuing France and sought to protect her independence and sovereignty. the most out of her duties to the ancient 'entente cordial'.

All in Europe agreed- they would no longer tolerate Hitler. Churchill became Prime Minister of Britain and became leader of the war effort, a task he was very much suited for.

According to the historian, Max Hastings, Germany, after facing a traumatising period when the western allies looked set to win, Germany made a formidable comeback and looked set for all intents and purposes to win. This short comeback proved not to last. The war lasted for six years until America and Russia which had changed its mind intervened in the war and assisted the western allies in winning the war effort. It is fair to say that without these two emerging superpowers, though later set to become rivals, both helped Europe to overcome the German threat. Russia lost the most troops out of all the allies.

The end of the war was determined by the meetings at Yalta and Potsdam where the likes of Churchill, Stalin, Degaulle of France and Roosevelt of America all discussed Germany's fate as rest as deciding how Europe and the world would be. It was decided that unlike the end of the first world war where the allies unduly harsh to Germany, Germany from now on be treated with greater fairness and compassion. It was agreed that the allies would do all they could to assist Germany to recover. It was agreed that the economic plan to be followed to assist Germany was the social market model, or the co-determination model which had origins in Catholic social teaching. Western Germany by and large followed this model, whilst eastern Europe under the control of Russia followed the communist model and hence lost out on the assistance of the allies.

Soon Europe became divided into West and East. Churchill in ever prescient mode predicted that Europe would be divided by what he termed an 'Iron Curtain' between the American West side of Europe and the Russian Eastern side of Europe of which the latter would heavily suffer. Churchill's warning proved correct. West Europe was for the most part under the control of the likes of America, Britain and France. America assisted western European countries with a substantive financial package known as the Marshall Plan.

Countries such as Britain chose and adopted America and her form of democracy, economic and social liberalism and free market capitalism in a bid to modernise and improve European society and Europe's economy. Others in mainland Europe such as France, Italy and Spain chose to follow the catholic church's social teaching model, known as the social market model otherwise known as the 'co-determination' model, which was also used in western Germany.

In terms of the eastern European countries, they were not so lucky as their western counterparts- for the next forty five years precisely they were to be governed by Russia which implemented a communist government on the countries of eastern Europe- unlike western Europe these countries had little freedom- most things were run by the state with little space for private sector enterprise.

At Yalta and Potsdam and other meetings, it was decided that the League of Nations would be shut down with a new supra-organisation replacing it, namely, the European Union, of which Germany became a member at first go, whilst others such as Britain joined later on after DeGaulle of France had prevented the UK from joining. The Union has proven to be a success and still exists in these modern times- even several members of the eastern bloc have joined it. Germany and France, two once sworn enemies during the war have become close and friendly allies and have come known as a faction in the Union as the 'German-Franco motor'. Germany has enjoyed a second renaissance with her economy in what has become known as the 'German miracle'. Germany regularly features in lists as one of the top performing economies in the world. As a sign of the recovery that Europe has made, she has enacted several treatises setting out her constitutional order and she even has a shared monetary currency, the Euro which has proven to be a success and has proven to be a competitive force amongst the likes of the American dollar and pound sterling. There is also free movement of people and a single trading bloc- free movement of goods and services.

America and Russia, after the war emerged as the two new superpowers on the global stage after the war, replacing the 'Great powers' of Britain and France. There was a Cold War between the two countries- the term 'cold' refers to the fact that there was no direct conflict between the two- the term refers to the fact that the two countries used other countries to engage in warfare, supporting them by financial and military means but that was far as it went. In short- it was war by proxy. It was now the era of nuclear weaponry- the world came close to a nuclear war with the Cuban Missile crisis where Russia had weapons in Cuba, whilst America had missiles in Italy and Turkey. After days of being at point of war, President JF Kennedy pronounced a cessation of all potential conflict. There were also wars in Tokyo, the Suez Crisis and the Hiroshima debacle.

Soon Soviet Russia began to loosen up and begin a new chapter in her history in which she would take a democratic turn- prior to that she had only known governance by monarchy or the dictatorial government usually and frequently associated with communism. She had a new leader, Mickael Gorbachev who was to prove a transformative leader in the history of Russia. Domestically, he governed by the terms of what he gave credence as 'glasnost' and 'perestroika'- 'openness' and 'transparency'. As president of Russia he ended the cold war. His policies led to Russia's looser grip on her soviet eastern bloc. During one night in 1990 Berlin city, Germany on the eastern side of a wall known as the Berlin wall that had been erected by soviet Russia to ban people from emigrating was pulled down and allowed the eastern inhabitants to have access the more hospitable and environmentally friendly west in a bid to be reunited with their families. Such policies have led the likes of the politics academic, Francis Fukuyama to note that these events were the end of different political ideologies and that all countries had reached or were about to reach an end point political ideology of political and social liberalism.

After 6 million of Jews had been killed in concentration camps during the war in what has become known as the holocaust in Germany by Hitler and Germany. Soon the Zionist cause became more popular where all countries now believed that it was time for the Jews to once again have a home land. Israel was to be protected and safeguarded by all countries and nations of good will and was to be assisted in terms of building a safe home for her citizens. Once again the problem of Jerusalem arose. All three religions- Christianity, Judaism and Islam in past life had claimed a stakehold to the territory- for Christianity- it was an area where Jesus whom they believed to be god incarnate journeyed there issuing and teaching parables. For the Jews, Jerusalem was the capital of Israel, where the once former Jews had enjoyed their home state of Israel before they became exiled. For those of the Islamic faith Jerusalem is the third holiest city after Mecca and Medina. Muslims believe that Muhammed was transported to Jerusalem during his Night Journey (Isra and Mi-raj). The Christians largely left the area. All agreed that there would be a Jewish state of Israel in order to welcome back and bring back the Jewish diaspora. Meanwhile the Islamic people known as Palestinians were given territory in the same country of Israel known as the West Bank and the Gaza Strip. The Palestinians were unhappy with the land that they received and believed they could not survive on the land with its poor environment and poor agriculture. Upon several times, the Palestinians engaged in wars with the Jewish people in Israel and on each and every account it has always lost land and lost territory. Even till this very day- things have not been resolved- at the moment of writing another war is going on between the Israelis and the Palestinians.

Since second world war, there has been no major wars concerning Europe- Europe is flourishing and is peaceful. The likes of French president Emmanuel Macron has proven to be a popular leader whilst the leader of the European Union, Ursula von Deleyen is also popular. Germany however is in a state of flux- she has lost a very popular and a very successful leader in Chancellor Angela Merkel- it remains to be seen with her new chancellor, Chancellor Olaf Scholz how he fares- it is still too early to embark on an evaluation of his policies and plans for Germany. There is also some tension elsewhere- for example the extremist Gert Wilders has been elected though people are concerned that he will cause problems as regards Holland's problems with Europe's accommodation of the Islamic people. Also President Putin is proving once again proving problematic with regard to his dealings with Ukraine in what has been a direct conflict.

Concluding Thoughts

Throughout this monograph I have narrated and detailed the events of what occurred in Germany- that is to say how the country emerged from debt following reparations imposed on it following the first world war, to how under the Hitler government the country achieved economic and social success. Hitler's government was full of ideas and full of plans as to how to fix the German economy- they knew what they were doing and were perfectly competent and adept.

However Hitler overreached himself- became greedy and overambitious- rather than respecting the individual sovereignty of all the European countries, as Fuhrer he believed almost in a made messianic manner that it fell to him and a few allies to save Europe- though what they were saving Europe from, no one knows.

The war lasted from 1939 to 1945- six years in total and two years more than the first war- 1914-1918.

Of course there have been over wars but none as bad as the second world war. Europe is pretty much united- she has her own supra-organisation, her own currency, her own trading bloc and her own executive, legislature and judiciary.

She even has own Bills of Rights- the European Convention of Human Rights and the Fundamental Chapter Social of Rights which contain a list of human and social rights that European citizens have.

One final thought. At the end of the war, a lot of help was given to Germany where she was enabled to emerge out of the mess that Hitler and his government left her in. However, no such help was given to Israel despite the fact that she lost 6 million of her people as a result of Germany's actions. Germany had not learnt her lesson. Having said that, there were the Nuremburg trials where members of the Nazi government were tried at court for their war crimes not only around the world, but especially concerning their treatment of the Jews. One could say that Germany was dealt with too lightly- there should have been tougher treatment in terms of dealing with her appalling treatment of the Jews.

Hence to conclude, the allies got it right- the second world war really was the war to end all wars. Europe has never looked back since and has enjoyed a renewed renaissance which has seen her as a social and economic superpower, rivalling other powers such as America and Russia. Whilst Europe is on very much friendly terms with America, relations with Russia remain fraught. However even her relations with Russia is beginning to improve- for example the likes of former Foreign Secretary David Miliband early on in his role noted that Russia as well as her former eastern soviet satellites could even join an expanded European Union. Europe's future and prospects look healthy- it remains to be seen just how successful she will be in the future.

POSTSCRIPT

PRIOR TO THE WAR, THERE WERE TWO COUNTRIES WERE believed to be 'global powers' or to put it in terms known through those days- 'Great Powers'. They were France and Great Britain.

Once the second world war had occurred, the two aforementioned countries, after the war lost their positions as global countries.

Instead, America and Russia took their place as global powers and became what was known as 'super powers'. America was revered for her entrance into the war and fast forewarding it through her military means and troop engagement. Russia too played a significant in the war- she lost around 27 million people during the war- almost half the entire total that passed away as a result of the atrocities.

These two powers which emerged, as a result of territorial gains were soon to engage in battle known as the 'Cold war'- war because they were in conflict with one another- intellectual, policy and strategy wise- 'cold' because at no time did they come into direct conflict with another militarily- instead the two- Russia and America supported other countries- financially, troops wise and arms wise in fighting each other on behalf of the two powers.

The British Prime Minister, Winston Churchill, in a speech in the House of Commons, anticipated that Russia would prove a threat to democratic countries across the global world which he called the 'Iron Curtain'.

Churchill was proved correct- Russia refused to move way from all of the countries she had so called liberated during the war- eastern Europe- they all fell under Stalin's communist control- the soviet bloc would remain until 1990, hen people broke down the Berlin wall and fled eastern Europe, most notably eastern Germany.

The issue at hand between America and Russia was that the democratic America feared that the communist Russia would have a malevolent influence over the territories she had captured especially in terms of imposing Marxist communism over them.

One of the first major crises was the Berlin Blockade of 1948 to 1949. In a bid to prove its dominance over its territorial gains, the Soviet union blocked the Western Allies' railway, road, and canal access to the sectors of Berlin under western control. The Soviets offered to renege on its past actions if the Westerners would withdraw its new Deutsche Mark from West Berlin. The western allies wanted to introduce a new currency in order to economically and assist west Germany in a bid to modernise her economy.

Millions of East Germans unhappy with their time under Soviet rule escaped to West Germany from East Germany, and Berlin became a major escape route. This led to a major power conflict over Berlin that stretched at least from 1946 to the construction of the Berlin wall in 1961. Eisenhower became American president in 1953 and Khrushchev became Soviet leader in the same year. The latter tried to push power on the former with little success. The Soviets back down when Eisenhower's promise bared the same resemblance as Truman's. When Truman was replaced by Kennedy in 1961, Khrushchev tried again, with essentially the same result.

After the war, China too witnessed a massive change in her style of governance. The scene was set between the nationalists status quo party and government against the Communists led by Mao Zedong.

America financed the large amounts of money and weapons to Chiang Kai-shek, who had previously ordered the 1927 massacre of Communists, splitting the country in a civil war. Meanwhile, Russia chose to support tbe Communists- they proved effective and efficient- they mobilised a massive army of peasants with their program of radical land reform and gradually began winning open battles against the KMT. In 1948 and 1949, the People's Liberation Army won three major campaigns that forced the nationalists government to retreat to Taiwan On 1 October 1948, Mao formally proclaimed the People's Republic of China. Even today, China remains to be a communist country, though, like Russia she has adopted a free market economic model of governance which is working, delivering high economic growth- rivalling the likes of America and Western Europe. Reports even note by in some time soon she will even outstrip the aforementioned and become the leading economic powerhouse in the world.

One event which saw the consecration and confirmation of America and Russia as the two superpowers of the world, and the humiliating downfall of Britain and France as former great powers, was the occurrence of the Suez Canal crisis. Israel invaded Egypt on 29 October 1956, because she wanted to reopen the blockade that the Egyptian President Nasser had issued an eight year blockade. Israel supported by its allies, France and Britain wanted to depose Egypt of her president and to regain control of the Suez Cana. All three allies were humiliated when America and Russia supported by the United Nations issued a declaration that the three- Israel, France and Britain, should withdraw from Egypt and respect her borders. The even is known as the UN's acknowledgment of America and Russia as two key major players in foreign affairs.

One event which occurred between America and Russia was the partitioning of Berlin with the creation of the Berlin wall. Khrushchev met up with Kennedy and sought to alert him as to the brain drain that Russia's eastern side of Germany was suffering from a brain drain with many leaving Est Germany to migrate to Western Germany and western Europe. A wall was built between western and easter Berlin, whilst Kennedy and Khrushchev agreed to remove all tanks reducing political and military tensions as a result.

One serious phase of the war occurred in 1962 with the Cuban Missile Crisis. It is known as the closes the two countries came close to facing one another militarily- not only that but facing each other with nuclear arms and missiles. America placed Japanese nuclear arms in Italy and Turkey- it also trained an army force of Cuban exiles, which the CIA led in an attempt to invade Cuba and overthrow its government. The Soviets were worried about the threat to a Cuban drift to China, which it had fractious relations with. In a series of meeting between Russia' Nikita Khrushchev and Fidel Castro of Cuba, they agreed to place nuclear missiles on Cuba to deter a future invasion. President Kennedy convened a meeting of the Executive Committee of the National Security Council (EXCOMM) but ignored their advice to carry out an air strike. Instead he chose a more moderate course by launching a naval blockade to prevent further missiles from going to Cuba.

The even happened 16 to 28 October 1962. Both Kennedy and Khrushchev signed an agreement that they would cease to prepare for warfare against one another by proxy.

The second of the Indochina Wars and a major conflict of the Cold War was the war between North Vietnam and South Vietnam, otherwise known as the Vietnam War- the north was supported by the Soviet Union, China, and other communist states, while the south was supported by the US and anti-communist allies. This made it, again, a proxy war between American and Russia. It lasted almost 20 years, with direct US military involvement ending in 1973. The war witnessed huge casualties- Vietnamese soldiers and civilians totalled approximately 970,000 to 3 million. Some 275,000-310,000 Cambodians, 20,000-62,000 Laotians whilst 58,220 US service members died. The US got what it wanted- after the war spilled into the Laotian and Cambodian civil wars, which ended the all three countries becoming communist by 1976.

The collapse of the Soviet Union in 1991 effectively ended the war. However one could note that the war is still ongoing-events such as where Russia has attacked Crimea and more recently Ukraine have shown that Russia has yet to learn her lesson of respecting the sovereignty of each country and the right and independence to govern her own countries has they see fit. Until she does so, then the global west will still remain ill at ease.

BIBLIOGRAPHY

Burleigh, Michael, The Third Reich, A New History

Stone, Norman, A Short WW11 History

Simms, Brendan, Hitler

Kershaw, Ian, Hitler

Bouverie, Tim, Appeasing Hitler

Hastings, Max, Armageddon

Caplan, Jane, Nazi Germany

www.ingramcontent.com/pod-product-compliance
Lightning Source LLC
Chambersburg PA
CBHW031417250726
48656CB00002B/714